MW00958997

ACE
THE INTERVIEW
SYSTEM

**The Job Search Blueprint for
Turning Interviews into Job Offers**

LINDSAY MUSTAIN

Copyright @ 2024 by Lindsay Mustain.

All rights reserved.

No portion of this publication may be reproduced, distributed, or transmitted in any form without written permission from the publisher or author, except as permitted by U.S. copyright law.Cover Design, Illustrations, and Interior Layout by Lindsay Mustain.

Disclaimer: The stories shared in this book are based on the author's personal recollections of events. To safeguard the privacy of the individuals mentioned, certain names, locations, and identifiable details have been altered. The author of this publication provides helpful information on job interviewing. However, this publication is not a definitive guide and does not replace a qualified professional, and there is no guarantee that the methods suggested in this book will be successful, owing to the risk that is involved in hiring actions of any kind. References are provided for informational purposes only and do not constitute endorsements of any websites or other sources. The publisher and author are not responsible for any actions you take or do not take as a result of reading this book, and any such liability is hereby expressly disclaimed. In the event you use any of the information in this book for yourself, the author and publisher assume no responsibility for your actions. Please note that websites listed in this publication may change or become obsolete.

To Jacob and Nora

I love you

Contents

Introduction

As I dropped my bags in my Airbnb in Boise, I looked down at my phone and saw a client had messaged me. "Can you talk?" she asked. My chest got tight, and my stomach felt queasy; no good conversation starts with those words. I was pretty new to being self-employed after leaving Amazon's talent acquisition team the year prior. I had enough coaching experience to know that my client Daphne needed some serious support at that moment. I quickly shot back a text: "I'll call you back in just a few minutes."

After taking a deep breath to center myself, I hit her number on my phone. When I heard Daphne's voice crack upon answering, I could tell the situation was not good. "What's going on?" I asked. The floodgates opened, and she sobbed as she explained the situation. Daphne had been looking for a job for a few months. She explained to me that, once again, another interview process had gone south. This had happened to her a few times in the six weeks we had been working together, and our key focus was now on closing the final stage of the job search

1

process: going from completing the interview to landing the job offer.

Daphne's issues had nothing to do with her experience. She was a well-qualified senior human resources leader who had a huge passion for making sure company culture and employee engagement were optimized to drive business results. She was savvy, experienced, and a quality candidate for the job. This was the fourth time in the last two weeks that an interview process had stalled out, and she was stuck in limbo. My heart broke as she asked "What's wrong with me? Why can't I find a job?" I'll tell you exactly what I told her: "There is nothing wrong with you. You are an incredible candidate. You have so much to offer an organization. I know it is scary now, but I promise that the right job is just around the corner."

Emotions in job searching run high, and it's easy to assume that everything you're doing at the moment is the problem. So, what was going wrong in Daphne's interviews?

I knew that I had already prepared Daphne to be successful through the final interview process. She had already done the work and improved her job search results, going from no interviews to multiple interview requests from different employers. At this stage, we were focusing on interview performance and showing up as what I call a "high caliber candidate" before, during, and after the interview had taken place. High caliber candidates are highly qualified individuals, understand how to present themselves as the **Candidate of Choice** throughout the interview process, and have cultivated a large demand for their time by having multiple companies interested in booking interviews. These candidates are perceived as the most valuable and companies will go to extreme lengths to close the deal, beat out their competition, and extend a job offer.

Daphne had done the hard part, but the waiting game can be excruciating. During this call, I was able to objectively evaluate the situation and gave Daphne the next steps to optimize her interview outcomes. Just four weeks later, she had three competitive job offers in hand.

Daphne was an experienced human resource leader, and it's easy for corporate America professionals like Daphne to fall into the trap of 'I should have known how to do this,' but the truth is that not many people know the best way to navigate a job search. It wasn't until after I had hired 10,343 people during my over 20 years in recruiting that I unlocked the secret sauce to acing the interview.

Back in 2001 when I landed my first recruiting responsibilities, things were quite different. The majority of applicants faxed or mailed in their resumes, and the large Seattle company I worked for didn't have an Applicant Tracking System (ATS). Over the next decade and a half, I grew my Fortune 500 talent acquisition experience and eventually was pursued by Amazon for four years before accepting a role at the corporate campus in Downtown Seattle. I worked on several projects for Amazon and I got well-known on LinkedIn for sharing my insights on how to increase your odds of success in job searching. Before I left in 2017, I was Amazon's most visible employee on the platform, getting more engagement than Amazon's profile or Jeff Bezos. Building a large following gave me a lot of career options inside of Amazon, and I was offered a unique opportunity to join a team where I'd lead talent acquisition strategies for some of the most elusive talent on the planet. Recruiting elusive talent, in reality, means there might be three people in the world who are qualified for a job, and it was my job to convince them to consider Amazon as their next career destination.

My biggest epiphany when working with elusive talent was how differently they navigated a job search. By default, they had additional power in the recruiting process as they were sought out by the company directly. When it came time to make a job offer, hiring managers would go to extreme lengths to close the deal. It was a much different experience than the average applicant who applies online and who generally will be sent a form email saying 'thanks but no thanks'.

The biggest question I asked myself: was there an easier way to navigate job interviews to turn them into job offers?

When I realized that the behavior of these elusive candidates was so uniquely different from the norm while they were closing job offers worth multiple six and seven figures, I reverse-engineered the process. The answer is yes; elusive talent and high caliber candidates behave radically different than the average job seeker. After my epiphany, I got highly invested in learning and disseminating these strategies to help other job seekers.

I shared some of these high caliber candidate strategies and insights using my platform on LinkedIn and in turn, started seeing incredible stories of success. Amazon wasn't as impressed and felt that I should keep some of these details to myself. Many times, I was told to remove the posts I shared on the platform, even though I knew these strategies could change the lives of many job seekers.

After having some deflating conversations with leaders at Amazon about helping optimize the process so candidates could have a better experience and have better results during our company's interview process, I decided that my talents were best served helping job seekers navigate the complex job searching process. In June 2017, I opened my business Talent Paradigm LLC. Since that time, my organization has worked with over 20,000 clients across 110 countries and six continents.

After analyzing our customer data, I was able to further refine the process of transforming job searches from fruitless to landing incredible opportunities with huge salary increases and I founded my proprietary system called Intentional Career Design in 2021. This was rocket fuel for our clients, and since introducing Intentional Career Design we've generated millions of dollars in salary increases.

Job markets are hyper-competitive right now, with the average job opening receiving 250 applications (Turczynski, 2022).

But here's the most amazing part: if you're landing job interviews, you've done the hardest part in the job search process so far. Getting to the point of any stage of an interview is typically reserved for just 10% of all candidates, giving you a significant advantage at this stage. At this point, it's all about optimizing your performance through the interview.

Inside my Intentional Career Design pathway is the blueprint for taking an interview request and turning it into a job offer. It's called the Ace the Interview System and this process has generated thousands of job offers and success stories for my clients. Through the rest of this book, I'll outline the step-by-step approach that will guide you in transforming your interviews into actual job offers to assist you in landing your dream career opportunity.

How this Book is Organized

Milestone I: Build Your Interview Acumen: Process Navigation and Mindset Mastery

In Milestone I, I'll share with you some of the biggest mindset makeovers you'll be making and give you a quick introduction to navigating the interview process successfully.

Milestone II: Mastering Interview Fundamentals

In Milestone II, I'll be covering the foundational aspects of interviewing well. These fundamentals are the basis we'll build the rest of the Ace the Interview System upon.

Milestone III: The Expert Interview Preparation Method

The key difference in predicting the outcomes of interviews can be determined by the level and depth of the preparation a candidate does. I'll share with you the expert methodology for interview preparation in this milestone.

Milestone IV: Decoding Interview Questions & Answers

This is the most robust section of the Ace the Interview System and I'll cover what interview questions to expect, how to answer them, and how to make the most powerful first impression.

Milestone V: Closing the Deal: Elevating Your Interview to Offer

The final stage of the Ace the Interview System is the specific approach for how to turn an interview into a job offer. I'll share with you how to strategically end the interview and how to follow-up and turn an interview into a real job opportunity.

This book is a powerful culmination of over twenty years of recruiting experience and from working with twenty thousand clients. I know that this will transform your interviews, so let's jump in!

Milestone I: Build Your Interview Acumen - Process Navigation and Mindset Mastery

" May the odds be ever in your favor. "
— Effie Trinket, The Hunger Games

Congratulations, you've embarked on a career ascension journey that most candidates will never know anything about. This is the shortcut to acing the interview process and landing lucrative job offers, despite anything that is happening in the economy and job market. Think of yourself as getting to see behind the scenes of corporate America's hiring practices... getting to sneak a peek at the proverbial recruiting wizard behind the curtain.

In many ways, the interviewing process feels like The Hunger Games. Many contenders are competing for one victorious prize; the job offer. There is a way to land on the proverbial platform in first place, and that starts with understanding the roadmap to navigate the broken hiring system. When you understand the realities of interviewing, you can allow yourself to use these shortcomings to increase your chance of success. One of the most important pieces of advice I can give you is that mindset in job searching is 80% of the game. Like Daphne, most job seekers will end up dejected and feeling broken when they come across setbacks because they don't understand that the system is inherently flawed. They'll get broken down and give up or settle on the path before they have the chance to reach the next summit of their career journey. You need to build your resiliency muscle to effectively job search. If you believe you are capable, willing to learn, do the work, and recognize that every no brings you closer to yes, you'll see the journey as an uphill climb that is a worthwhile pursuit.

The knowledge I share with you is game-changing. My background includes real-life corporate recruiting experience and career coaching. This unique perspective allows me to share the realities of the landscape of the interview process and teach you how to hack job searching to help you turn your interviews into job offers. There is only one thing that I can assure you that will revolutionize your interview results, and that's to do the work. Trust the process, take action, and you'll be well prepared to ace any interview. Let's get started.

Chapter 1: Interview Process Flaws - Navigating a Broken System

In this chapter, I will be diving headfirst into the world of corporate interviews, and uncovering the inherent flaws and inconsistencies within the traditional interview process. My goal for you in reading this chapter is to gain a fresh perspective on the purpose of interviews, learn how to navigate the interview process successfully, and leverage your interview performance to land competitive job offers. You play an active role in directly influencing the outcome of your interview by combining strategic actions and checking your mindset.

Standing Among Top Candidates

If you've been asked to interview for a job... let me be the first to congratulate you! Making it to the interview stage means you are part of the top 10% of all candidates who expressed interest in a job opportunity. Ultimately, it's a big deal and you are in a significant position of advantage in the hiring process. Keep this in mind as we move forward – you have already beaten out 90% of other applicants.

Understanding Interview Stakes

While you've already beaten out 90% of candidates, remember that interviews hold no real stakes as the interviewee. Many times, I see candidates losing their cool, stressing out, and fretting themselves into a worried mess about an interview. Yes, the outcome holds importance, but you need to adopt a mindset of detachment. Whether the interview goes well or not, you possess the same skills, qualifications, and experience that got you there in the first place. Instead of hoping that a company 'picks you', I want you to reframe into the mindset of "we'll see if this is an opportunity that's worthy of my expertise and energy". This is a much more powerful position to walk into an interview with and eliminates the needy style energy most candidates bring to interviews.

Unlocking High Performance Strategies: Minimizing Bias and Maximizing Opportunities

The focus of this book is centered on high performance interview strategies. My overall objective is to teach you how to use the broken interview system to our advantage and navigate the interview process with confidence. I want to equip you with recruiting industry knowledge and tools to minimize human bias, offer psychological hacks to tilt the odds and increase your chances of securing a job offer, to then help you negotiate from a position of strength.

Spoiler: Most Interviewers Are Bad Interviewers

If you've ever interviewed for a job... you probably know this to be true. Most interviewers lack the critical skills to interview candidates effectively. Interview processes are varied, and there is little consistency, both between companies and teams. It's essential not to take the outcome of an interview personally. A great deal of the process depends on the interviewer's judgment and ability. Inside this book, I'm going to show you exactly how to navigate these challenges and strategize around these inconsistencies.

Job Interviews Do Not Predict On-the-Job Performance

Did you know that job interviews do a poor job of predicting on-the-job performance accurately? This powerful insight is an invitation for you to hack the system. Throughout this book, I will uncover and reveal more flaws in the interview process and help you to develop strategies to present yourself as a top-tier candidate that eliminates the competition.

Welcome to the Ace the Interview System: Hacking the Traditional Process

Let me introduce you to the Ace the Interview System – a powerful methodology designed to hack the traditional job interview process. The remainder of this book will walk through the Ace the Interview System step-by-step and you'll learn exactly how to position yourself as a high caliber candidate and which in turn, opens many doors to securing multiple job offers. Get ready to transform the way you approach interviews and secure the opportunities you truly deserve.

Milestone II: Mastering Interview Fundamentals

"Get the fundamentals down and the level of everything you do will rise."
— *Michael Jordan*

Kari had applied to 176 jobs and while she had gotten a small handful of responses, the last consulting job interview she had received had put her in tears afterward. She knew she was well qualified to do the job, but it felt like she'd be selling her soul just to make a paycheck. Even though Kari held a Ph.D., she didn't know how to combine the pursuit of both her passion and the desire to perform meaningful work to find work that really mattered. When we started working together, we had to deprogram some of the narratives around the fundamentals of job searches and interviewing. Along her journey, she got multiple competitive offers, including an education-based position that went on a bidding war to get her to come on board. Understanding the basics is the foundation of a successful interview. After working with Kari for just a couple of months, she exclaimed "You can do what you love and you can get paid for it; I just got a 44% increase in salary!"

You might feel inclined to overlook this chapter in the context of job interviews. However, doing so would be a mistake, as the quality of your interviews will be directly attributed to how well you understand and master the fundamentals.

In this chapter, I'm going to reveal some of the secrets that are only shared with my mastermind, where I teach my clients how to secure six-figure pay increases. If that's not a reason to pay attention to this chapter, I don't know what is. Throughout the chapters in Milestone II, I will explore how to elevate your technique and adopt a strategic approach to interviewing.As mentioned in Milestone I, 80% of your success in interviews lies within your mindset. Your mindset sets the tone for the entire interview process. It is crucial to create and nurture positive thoughts, empowering mantras, and beliefs about your worthiness as a candidate. When you have the belief that you are a quality candidate and your actions align with that belief, you will be able to successfully convey your confidence to potential employers and create a powerful first impression. You'll also in turn strengthen your resiliency muscle. These attributes are foundational in reshaping your interview outcomes.

The techniques that I cover in this milestone combine both mindset and knowledge so you can more easily navigate the interviewing process. Mastering interview fundamentals and combining it with the knowledge of the interview process allows you to be better equipped to navigate your job search and see a massive upgrade to the outcomes of your interviews.

Let's jump in and dive deeper into the aspects of strategic interviewing and navigating different interview structures and formats.

Chapter 2: Strategic Interviewing - The Recruiter's Guide to Elevate Your Technique

Job interviewing often brings along a bundle of stress and a landscape of unknowns. Hiring over 10,000 professionals in corporate America gives me a unique vantage point to share with you what top talent does to distinguish themselves from the average job seeker. There's a lot of bad advice out here, so let me guide you through positioning yourself as top talent and avoiding the pitfalls that even the most seasoned individuals can stumble upon.

Always Show Up At Your Best

Many times my coaching clients will ask how to make sure their experience matches what the interviewer is looking for. This is the wrong question to be asking. Instead, ask yourself, how do I show up as the best professional version of myself? When a company has an open headcount, you should perceive that opening is for a position on a specific team. It's not un-common for a hiring manager to upgrade or downgrade a role to suit the perfect candidate. Instead of trying to fit yourself into the job description box, show up at your best and highest level, and don't shy away from demonstrating the impact and scope of the experience and accomplishments you have. My clients frequently tell me stories of having a role re-graded (meaning to a higher pay grade) once they demonstrate their expertise. Don't dumb down your experience just because the position posted is not the same level as you desire.

Almost everything in hiring a new position is up for nego-tiation. Money, title, working location, and job description – these are all negotiable factors in the hiring process. It's crucial to assert your needs and desires and be willing to say no if a company is not in alignment with your values or treats you poorly.

First Impressions Matter Most

Did you know that interviewers often make subconscious decisions within the first thirty seconds of meeting a candidate? This unconscious bias happens quickly and it's based solely on your first impression (Renne, 2018). This is called anchor bias, and it means that humans give more weight to the initial piece of information they gather in a decision-making process (Furnham & Boo, 2011). Be sure you make a positive first impression with your interviewer; focus on being warm, inviting, and confident as this impression will be weighted more heavily than any other part of your interview.

Likeability Trumps Experience

The most qualified candidate doesn't always land the job. This is one of the most important lessons I can share with you after 20 years in the Human Resources field. When a hiring manager is deciding whether to hire you, they're not going to solely use your experience and education as the benchmark for hiring. Post-interview, the recruiter for the position will reach out to the hiring manager to ask one question: "Did you like them?" Not "Are they the most qualified person for the job?" While expertise is important, what matters most is likeability. It's whether or not they 'like' you, and they feel you will have a good 'fit' on the team.

When we reject candidates because they weren't the 'right fit', what they mean is that you didn't win the likeability factor with the hiring manager and there's a concern about whether or not you will fit in with the team dynamic. Always focus on building rapport in your interview first and then cement that positive first impression with demonstrable expertise and results.

The Waiting Game: Navigating Uncertainty

The time after an interview can be filled with anxiety and self-doubt and it's natural to feel anxious for a decision during the waiting period. Avoid replaying every detail of the interview or dwelling on perceived missteps. Instead, focus on activities that increase your worthiness and remind you of your value.

If a hiring manager intends to reject your candidacy after the interview, they will not spend a lot of time waiting around to do so. If you're not a good fit, you'll likely see that update come quickly. If you're still waiting on hearing results, you're likely a 'yes' or a 'maybe', so stay positive and keep cultivating new interview opportunities.

One of my favorite ways to combat anxiety around interviewing results is to create a gratitude practice. Focus on what you can be grateful for, even if it is just the ability to read this sentence. List out everything, big or small, that you can have to be grateful for. This powerful reframe can move you from a place of fear to a place of gratitude.

Rejection is Redirection

If you're job searching, there's one thing I can guarantee one thing that will happen on your journey. It's that you're going to be rejected from opportunities that appear amazing and perfectly suited to your skill set. For most candidates, getting the rejection email (or being ghosted) in the interview process leaves you feeling defeated and demoralized. You might wonder if you've got what it takes or if something is wrong with you. I promise you that you are worthy and absolutely nothing is wrong with you. The harsh reality is that not every job opportunity will result in an offer. During my recruiting career, I rejected over 99% of all candidates, most of which were amazing individuals with incredible talent. You must understand that rejection is a necessary part of job searching and you need to create a game plan for handling rejection. The absolute worst outcome is that rejection stops you in your job search and causes you to lose hope or give up on pursuing your career aspirations. I want you to remember that every "no" we encounter brings you one step closer to a resounding "yes." Instead of letting rejection paralyze you, use it as fuel to improve and push forward, knowing that each setback is just a detour on your path to landing a dream job opportunity. Remember, a rejection is not a reflection of your worth as a candidate - it's merely a part of the process.

Resilience and Self-Worth

One of the most important aspects of bouncing back from rejection is understanding your worthiness. If you want to navigate the interview process successfully, you must have a strong sense of self-worth. It's crucial to understand that your worthiness is not determined by one person's opinion of you. No matter the outcome of an interview or any perceived failure, your worth as a candidate remains unchanged. You are talented, skilled, and deserving of opportunities. When you get the wobbles in your job search, take time to remind yourself of your worth and believe in it wholeheartedly. If you don't believe you're worthy, neither will the interviewer. Hold your head high and know that your skills, experiences, and unique attributes are assets that make you a standout candidate.

Creating Leverage as a High Caliber Candidate

People want what they can't have. This especially applies to job candidates. I've seen hiring managers bend over backward for candidates who have multiple companies pursuing them. Why is this? Because it increases the perception of the candidate's value and people don't want to miss out and let the perfect hire slip through their fingers. One of the most important aspects of showing up as a high caliber candidate is to have leverage in the process by having multiple options and opportunities at play. When you're job searching, accept most of the interviews that are offered to you. Even if an opportunity doesn't seem perfect on paper, it's important to seize every interview chance that comes your way. Don't dismiss an interview simply because it doesn't seem like the perfect fit. I recommend you strive for the 80% rule; if it matches 80% of your desires in your next career opportunity, take the time to do the interview. Remember that interview practice is costly, so seize every chance, especially when the stakes are lower. Every interview is an opportunity for practice and growth, and being in demand for interviews increases your perception of being top talent. By continually engaging in the interview process, you create more leverage and increase the likelihood of receiving multiple job offers. Don't limit yourself by fixating on a single opportunity, no matter how promising or attractive; until a job offer is signed, a background check is passed, and a start date has been confirmed. Despite a company's best intentions, positions can be eliminated and job offers may fall through. High caliber candidates are always in demand, so I recommend you always take a proactive approach to your career and continuously seek out and accept new opportunities that can elevate your position.

A high caliber candidate has multiple career opportunities and they tend to land multiple job offers. Because they are so high in demand, companies compete for them because they are perceived to be 'top talent'; this is the most desirable position we can be in as candidates as we can leverage this position in negotiations for our next role. This may mean companies will compete against one another to offer the best job title/salary, while you get the opportunity to choose what's best for your career goals.

Permission to Decline Job Offers

I give you permission to say no to any job offer that you're offered. Not every position is the right one for your career, your family, or your values. When you need a job, it can be pretty tempting to take any offer that comes your way and sacrifice what matters most to you and your family. Be sure to view any job offer objectively; determine if it's first a match for what you want to be doing in your career, how it will benefit you and your family, and if you're choosing because it's the right opportunity or from fear. I promise that there are dozens of other opportunities out there that will be lucky to have you, as long as you are willing to do the work to cultivate them. Choose from abundance, and not scarcity. You are worthy of having a job you love at a company that values you.

Milestone III: The Expert Interview Preparation Method

 "Luck is what happens when preparation meets opportunity." — Seneca

The bottom line, preparation is the key to completing an interview and landing a job offer. After spending over two decades in talent acquisition, I can confidently say that successful interviews are 100% dependent on how well you prepare. Interview preparation is much more than just a basic skim of the company's website; your job is to connect the dots between what the company is hiring for and what you bring to the table.

During my time at Amazon, my team's success rate from an onsite interview to a job offer was pretty dismal even though we were working with senior level professionals and executives.

The metrics showed that teamwide, less than 50% of candidates were extended a job offer; however, my inclination rate was consistently at 75% or higher. This meant it took fewer candidates and less interviewer time to get to a better result. We took my interviewing preparation best practices and extended them to be the standard process for our team; this small shift raised the collective inclination rate to over 70%. The Interview Preparation Playbook in Chapter 4 is the cumulation of all the best strategies, insights, and skills that I've assembled that will help you to nail the interview. It's important to point out that successfully making it through the interview process has nothing to do with luck; it all comes down to your dedication to preparing yourself for the interview.

The core difference between moving forward in the interview process and/or being offered a job opportunity truly comes down to your level of preparation. Milestone III will challenge you to critically evaluate your interview preparation in new ways.

We'll focus on:

- Going deep into business research beyond the basics

- Helping you identify the needs of the organization and matching the skills you have

- Learning how and where to gather interviewer-specific

information to help you build rapport and a lasting impression

- Understanding the key elements you'll need to prepare successfully to pass the interview and move on to the next step

I can assure you that using this playbook has dramatically helped my clients and candidates transform their job search results. Keep your mind open as I share with you the strategies included in my playbook to help you optimize your interview preparation.

Chapter 3: Navigating the Process - Interview Structure and Formats

I t's exciting when you land an interview but it's also usually a nerve-racking moment. Things have changed a lot in the way interviews happen over the last decade. In this chapter, I'm here to guide you through the current interview styles commonly seen in corporate America. This chapter focuses on interview structure and format fundamentals. We'll be taking a closer look at interview processes, how these interviews are structured, and the reasons they're done this way. I'll be sharing some knowledge and insider tips on how to successfully navigate each type of interview format.

1st Round Interviews: The Phone Interview

Also known as the phone screen, this is the typical introductory step in the interview process after confirming you meet the qualifications of the role. The phone interview has one purpose: to assess your competency and determine if you're a suitable fit for the role and the hiring manager. When the recruiter or interviewer first reaches out to you, respond quickly and try to book the first available interview time. In my experience, top talent consistently is proactive, quick to respond, and books the first available appointment time. When it comes time to interview, enthusiasm is your secret sauce. Remember, a smile can be heard through your voice. Enthusiasm trumps expertise at this stage. This interview is not just about showcasing your skills; it's about demonstrating your excitement for the opportunity at hand. This interview is typically no more than 45 minutes, and if you run over on time, take it as a good sign. The company's goal of this interview is to tell you more about the company and the opportunity, and then confirm that you have the experience and are a good match for the opportunity, manager, and culture.

In some companies, virtual interviews, whether a live video interview or an on-demand interview, have taken the place of the phone interview. I've included details below in this chapter on virtual interviews. Once you have passed the phone interview or its equivalent, you'll be moved on to the 2nd round of interviews.

There are many times when you might bring all the right experience to the table that a job description lists, but behind the scenes, there may be unlisted preferred qualifications that the hiring manager desires. Don't let that dissuade you from making a great impression and building a relationship with the recruiter as they frequently keep lists of top candidates that would be a good fit for other company opportunities.

2nd Round Interviews: Hiring Manager Interview

If you've successfully passed the phone screening with the first interviewer, it's very common to have your following interview directly with the hiring manager. In this interview, they're going to assess your competency at a much deeper level than the phone screen with the recruiter/interviewer. The biggest goal of this interview is to 1) determine if you have the expertise to be successful in completing the requirements of the job and 2) decide if you are a good fit to work well with the hiring manager and their team. This interview can be between 30 and 60 minutes and may take place over the phone, in a video/virtual interview, and occasionally on-site. It's also worth noting that if the quality of your phone screen is high, you may skip over to the stakeholder/panel interview stage.

2nd Round Interviews: Stakeholder and Panel Interviews

Only after you've passed the phone screen and the hiring manager feels you are a good fit for the role will you be scheduled with the team. While it can be a bit nerve-racking to prepare for an interview loop (a series of interviews with a single company), this is a great sign that you're seriously in the running for this job opportunity.

When a candidate reaches the second stage of the interview process, there is typically an interview loop which can be held in person or virtually. Brace yourself for various interview styles, from behavioral questions to technical assessments. Some interview loops can be extensive, with multiple interviews lasting from a couple of hours to a couple of days. When you reach this stage, you're typically up against one to five other people meaning that there is less competition. Being prepared for each interview is a game changer for distinguishing yourself as top talent among the remainder of the other candidates.

Stakeholder interviews are any type of interview that is held with a party outside of the recruiter and the hiring manager. Stakeholders are typically people in leadership positions or they may be people in positions that will frequently interact with this new hire including the position's peers. Stakeholder interviews can be panel interviews with multiple interviewers including the hiring manager. While peers' opinions can influence the decision, they typically don't have the authority to veto or approve a candidate. Their input helps the hiring manager gain a more holistic perspective. Be wary of interview processes that include more than five stakeholders as this can indicate a slower hiring process and reflect that the company does not empower hiring managers to make their own hiring decisions.

For technically aligned roles, you should be prepared for a technical assessment or simulation as part of the interview process. These assessments, while stressful, are an opportunity to showcase your technical expertise, problem-solving skills, and your ability to work under pressure. Be prepared to be tested on your knowledge and real-world application of job-specific technical ability.

Final Round Interviews

Congratulations! You've made it to the final interview stage. This is where the competition intensifies, and your chances of getting the job are at their highest. Remember, not getting the job doesn't necessarily mean there is something wrong with you. There may be other factors involved, such as a better fit or specific qualifications required. When you make it to the final interview stage, prepare to meet with the most senior leader(s) involved in the interview process. Typically this interview is more brief and is only there to ensure the leader is on board and approves the final hiring decision.

Embracing New Technology: On-Demand Virtual Interviews/Live Video Interviews

One of the newest innovations in the recruiting industry has been the video interview. Video interviews can happen either on-demand (meaning you record your answers at your convenience) or live with the interviewer(s). As with phone interviews, quick responses for a live video interview or on demand video interview can impact your candidacy so complete these requests as soon as you are able. Hiring managers frequently use video screening to complete the interview process more quickly and to remove travel barriers for long-distance candidates and/or interviewers. Many candidates get worried with on demand video interviews, but expect to see this trend continue to grow. I'm a fan of on demand virtual interviews as it lets me quickly hear back from top candidates and experience their enthusiasm for the opportunity firsthand while getting to know their experience more deeply than the resume can explain in a quick review. The best way to ace the video interview is to practice on camera; record and review your responses before you're scheduled for the video interview. You can prepare easily by answering some of the top interview questions in Chapter 7 while in a virtual meeting or using the video function on a smartphone.

Lack of Consistency in the Hiring Process

In the world of job interviews, there's little consistency between companies and teams, but now you are more prepared with the knowledge to successfully navigate any process. From phone screens to video interviews, stakeholder interviews, and finally, the in-person meeting, the interview styles used are diverse. Be prepared for any interview format, and remember, success lies not only in proving your competence but also in showcasing your genuine enthusiasm.

Waiting for Next Steps & Ghosting

Sadly, there are many times in the interview process when there will be delays. Most of these delays are due to interviewing other candidates though in some cases, it is a case of delays because the company is unsure of what they want to do next in the hiring process. Do not take this as a poor reflection of your candidacy; it happens in every company I've ever worked with and after supporting over 20,000 clients, I can assure you that you are not alone. In Chapters 11 and 12, I'll show you how to help improve your odds of hearing back and how to properly follow up.

Reminder: Rejection is Redirection

I've mentioned this in Chapter 2, but it's worth repeating. Not moving forward in the interview process and not being selected for an opportunity is not a reflection of the worth you bring to the table. Remain objective and seek out feedback (more about this in Chapter 12), and determine how you can improve. The absolute best way to keep the stakes low for any interview is by cultivating multiple job interviews so you have the luxury of choosing what career opportunity you want most; rather than feeling powerless and dejected in the process when a single job doesn't work out. Keep going; you're worth it!

Chapter 4: The Interview Preparation Playbook

I've hired 10,343 people in my corporate recruiting career, and I've witnessed some of the most incredible interviews that have blown me away and also had a front row seat to some epic interview disasters. Most candidates tend to fall right in the middle, being easily forgotten and quickly declined because they didn't know how to stand apart from the crowd. The next few chapters are focused on unveiling my personal strategies that help my clients beat out other candidates in the process and win job offers from the most prestigious and competitive interviewing processes that exist today.

Step 1: Cracking the Company Code: Strategic Organizational Research

The quickest way to lose out on a career opportunity is by not doing your homework on the organization you'll be interviewing with. The first step in our interview preparation playbook begins with researching the company. I call this business intelligence gathering, and it's what sets apart high potential talent from other candidates. I'm looking for more than just basic information on the company that you would find on the organization's website. I want you to dig deeper to uncover the information about the business and connect the dots between what the company requires and what you as a candidate offer to solve those needs. Your goal is to extensively research the organization focusing on a SWOT analysis. If you're not familiar with a SWOT analysis, this acronym stands for Strengths, Weaknesses, Opportunities, and Threats. Take a critical problem-solving approach to investigate the company's goals, challenges, where they're being successful, and where they are struggling. Then determine how your skill set can solve the challenges and gaps they have. Your goal is to showcase your candidacy as the perfect solution for the requirements they're hiring for.

One of the most common questions you'll face during the interview process is 'Why do you want to work here?' or 'What interests you in this position?' Use your research to create a bespoke and strategic answer that is truly unique by combining your expertise with how you can help the organization achieve its goals. This is a game changer that will immediately set you apart from other candidates.

Where to look to find organization-specific business intelligence:

- Company website

  - Home page

  - About us page

    - Mission and values

    - Company history

  - Career page/site

  - Investor relations

    - Earning statements/annual reports

    - Shareholder calls

    - Press releases

- Company social media

  - LinkedIn page

- Twitter/X

- Facebook

- YouTube

- Instagram

• Company culture evaluation

- Glassdoor

- Indeed

- The Muse

- Salary.com

After you have researched the organization, take the process even further by researching the interviewer(s) you'll be meeting with so you can connect better and impress them immediately with your knowledge. Dig deep into the interviewer's background, education, time with the current company, and any notable experience or interests that are relevant to you and/or the opportunity.

<u>Where to look to find interviewer-specific information:</u>

- LinkedIn profile

  - Look for shared connections and people you're both connected to. Feel free to contact anyone you know that may also know your interviewer to ask for advice when meeting with them. Taking these added steps can help build rapport and give you the benefit of an increased reputation.

- Twitter/X

- Facebook

- Instagram

- Google search engine

  - Articles they've written or been quoted in

  - Podcasts/interviews they've recorded

  - Hobbies/interests

  - Awards/recognition

  - Passion projects

    - Boards they serve on

- Professional memberships

- Volunteer work

By researching your interviewer, you can use this knowledge in your interview to build rapport and share affinities, interests, and similar experiences.

Step 2: Prepare Your Interview Answer Vault

One of the trickiest challenges that stumbles even the most qualified candidates is getting stuck on answering an interview question. The easiest way to help yourself with this predicament is to prepare a set of key answers in advance. That way, when the moment arises for you to answer a question, you will be ready to pull out a strategic answer that highlights your qualities as a top candidate.

Key Areas to Prepare:

- Elevator Pitch

    - The elevator pitch is the most critical 90 seconds of your interview and it's asked in over 90% of all interviews. As your interview begins, the interviewer will unconsciously decide whether or not you're a good fit for the job.

- First impressions matter and anchor bias is at work so optimize your interview success chances by crafting a compelling elevator pitch and having it memorized and ready to deliver the moment the interview starts (Furnham & Boo, 2011). I'll cover the ideal framework for your perfect elevator pitch in Chapter 8.

- Resume Walkthrough

  - Being able to clearly explain your work history is a challenge for most candidates. It gets especially tricky when explaining gaps or reasons you left a job (more on this in Chapter 9). Be sure you have a clear idea of each job and the highlights you include on your resume. Be prepared to showcase your results and accomplishments throughout your employment history, rather than your tasks and general responsibilities.

- Work Examples for Interview Questions

  - You'll want to prepare for the interview questions you'll be asked by selecting some examples from your work history that demonstrate your level of experience and excellence. Having examples that you have already selected minimizes those moments of forgetfulness and on-the-spot anxiety. This is key to optimizing your interview results.

- Questions for Your Interviewer

  ○ One of the most missed opportunities in the interview process is the chance to ask questions at the end. This is not the time to ask tactical questions, but instead a chance to cement your standing as top talent by asking questions that help your interviewer understand that you have the skills needed to be successful in the job.

You might be wondering exactly how to pull each of these four areas off and I promise I've got you covered. I'll discuss each of these topics more deeply and show you how to prepare for the critical interview moments inside Milestones IV and V.

Step 3: Dress for Success

You never get a second chance to make a first impression. We've all heard this adage and it's especially true when it comes to interviews in corporate America. The first thirty seconds are crucial when meeting someone for the first time (Furnham & Boo, 2011). During this time we form our baseline opinion of someone, which is why your first impression directly impacts how successful your interview will be. I must remind you that the full goal of this book is to help you successfully pass the interview process and land job offers. One key component to going further in the interview process is to minimize any biases against you. Sometimes people feel very strongly about representing their personal style in an interview. While I understand that desire, I want you to contemplate how you can reduce biases that can penalize you and also how to implement the best practice for dressing appropriately for an interview.

As a recruiter, one of the key points I always cover with candidates who are in the interviewer-facing stage of their interview process is how to dress for the interview. Keep in mind that the best resource you have when interviewing is the recruiter for the job opening. It's in the recruiter's best interest to help their candidates be successful during the interview process so feel free to contact them to get more information.

Here are some guidelines on how to make the best first impression:

- Always dress professionally

    ◦ This seems obvious, but I've seen candidates show up in athletic gear, club wear, and shorts. Dress conservatively in clean, ironed, or pressed clothing free of wrinkles.

- Industry-standard interviewing attire is usually a version of a business suit. I'd recommend having slacks and/or a skirt, a suit jacket, a dress shirt, and closed-toe shoes for your interviews.

  - The most influential colors to wear are black, gray, brown, and navy. Neutral colors are best to create a positive impression when meeting your interviewer.

- In some workplaces (especially in high-tech), interviewing in jeans and sneakers may be appropriate. Be sure to ask your recruiter for guidance because this is an exception to the rule.

- Dress one level up from the workplace dress code

  - For example, if the dress code is business casual, dress to a business professional level and wear a suit jacket and/or tie. It's always better to be overdressed than underdressed during an interview.

- Be minimal and keep it clean

  - Less is more. Think minimally when it comes to hair, jewelry, makeup, and nails. Facial hair should be well groomed. Practice good hygiene.

- Dress from head to toe

  - In a world where so many interviews are held virtually, don't just dress from the waist up. I've heard too many stories where candidates had to stand up unexpectedly and while they were business up top, they were sporting pajama pants or shorts on the bottom.

- Skip the perfume/cologne

  - With so many allergies and people who struggle with the smell of fragrances, I recommend you avoid it completely and instead plan on showing up fresh from the shower.

- Invest in a padfolio/calendar

  - In my experience, candidates who carry a padfolio/calendar are perceived as consummate professionals who are better qualified, more prepared, and typically have more favorable outcomes. This is an easy way to tip the interview scales in your favor.

Psychology-Backed Interview Strategies for Likeability and Confidence

Preparing for an interview goes beyond researching and dressing the part. To get the best results, you can focus on mindset and psychological hacks. Using these strategies in an interview can assist you with absolutely nailing the interview, be perceived as top talent, and landing the job offer.

The Power of Mindset

Here's your reminder that people want what they can't have. When something is in demand, it is perceived to be more valuable. In the context of an interview, so many candidates focus on being 'lucky' to be considered for the opportunity and are desperate to land the job. This comes off as validation-seeking (or 'pick me') behavior that repels your ideal career opportunity. Focus on showing enthusiasm for the opportunity while balancing what you can provide to the employer as their newest hire. When you switch the focus from 'pick me' to 'we'll see if this is an opportunity that is worthy of me' you change your power position. You're not open to any job; you're open to the right job. You're not tied to this opportunity; instead, you have a multitude of options and are exploring whether this job and employer are the right fit for your next career move. Do you see and feel the difference between the contrast of those statements?

This is called increasing your power position. When you inherently know that you are valuable and worthy, you show up with a level of confidence that other candidates just don't bring to the table. Focus on being detached from the outcome and showing up at your best. You've got lots of options, and any company interviewing you would be lucky to have you.

Body Language and the Power of Mirroring

Nonverbal communication is the most important part of an interview; it matters even more than your words. When your body language matches your words, you increase trust, confidence, and likability. Always keep your body language open (no crossed arms), and face your interviewer(s). You can take this to the next level by subtly mirroring your interviewer's body language throughout the interview. This little-known psychological hack can help create a sense of connection and camaraderie that builds a more positive atmosphere in the interview and increases your perception of likability.

Strike a Power Pose

One of my favorite tricks to feel more confident before walking into an important meeting or presenting in front of an audience is using a power pose. I learned this technique from a TED talk by Amy Cuddy and while this area is undergoing additional research, I can personally attest that this technique has assisted me in feeling more composed and powerful before walking into a higher-stakes environment (Cuddy, 2012). Adopt a Wonder Woman or Superman pose by standing hips-width apart placing your hands on your hips for 120 seconds. We perform this pose before the interview, so take the pose in a bathroom or a meeting room before your interviewer arrives. When the interview starts, bring this power and confidence into your conversation and use it to enhance your first impression.

Demonstrate Confidence with Eye Contact

Our body language silently communicates how we feel. If we show up in an interview hunched over, making little eye contact, and mumbling our words, an interviewer could perceive you are disinterested, bored, combative, and/or unqualified. Instead, focus on appearing calm, confident, prepared, centered, and engaged. One of the biggest struggles candidates have in interviewing is making eye contact. The question is, when do we do it and when is it too much? The easiest answer to this is to follow the leader. People inherently like what is like themselves. So model the interviewer's behavior. If they're making eye contact, you should make eye contact. If they're looking away, you should also break eye contact. Each person has a threshold for what feels good regarding the amount of eye contact they receive; this approach allows you to adjust the level of intensity of eye contact for the individual.

Pacing Your Answers

It's perfectly normal to feel nervous while interviewing. Many times, this anxiety can creep in and cause us to rush through our interview answers and conversations. I want you to approach your interview answers similarly to the way you approach eye contact. The pace of your answers should match the pace of the interviewer, just slightly faster. I've been told many times that I speak too quickly, so you need to know your audience here. Model the pace at which they ask your interview question. You should be slightly faster than them and focus on being concise. I'll help you understand exactly how to answer interview questions in Chapter 9, but for now focus on modeling the pace of the interviewer, being concise and to the point, and allowing the interviewer to have the chance to ask you follow-up questions.

The next part of the book is where we will do the heavy lifting; it's where we optimize your interview performance so you can start turning interviews into job offers. I'm excited to share some of my favorite frameworks for interview success so let's jump in!

Milestone IV: Decoding Interview Questions & Answers

 "Nothing worth having comes easy." — Theodore Roosevelt

Rebecca wanted to pivot her career into artificial intelligence (AI) but got typecast in her current career of data management and enterprise resource planning. After focusing on her strengths and aptitudes she already possessed that translated directly into AI, she started to land interviews, but the heavy lifting came down to convincing the interviewer she was the best candidate for the job in a field she had never worked in.

I'll never forget the moment we were recapping a recent interview opportunity and she described how she started her interview with my proprietary framework called the Perfect Elevator Pitch. "After I finished my elevator pitch, my interviewer's jaw dropped. She leaned in and instead of a traditional interview, we had a conversation about my background. I was able to answer her questions using the Super STAR technique and closed the interview exactly like we discussed. She said I should hear back by the end of the day tomorrow." I was delighted to hear how it had gone, and asked her to update me when she was contacted by the interviewer. The next message that popped up from this client confirmed she had been extended a job offer and the last time I checked in with her, she had increased her salary by 500% since we started working together. It's not the first time I've seen incredible job offers come from following the processes I cover in this milestone, and I'm thrilled to share this technique with you to use in your next interview.

This milestone, by far, is the most meaty and important to interview success and it's the heart and soul of the book. It's also worth noting that some readers may be tempted to jump in and start with the chapters in Milestone IV. Therefore, it's important to point out that your success will not come down to only answering the questions effectively; it's a combination of interview preparation and strategically closing the interview process. If you want the absolute best results, please take the time to go through this book cover to cover. The methods I share in these chapters are brought to you after distilling millions of data points from both my recruiting career and working with tens of thousands of clients and turning them into proven strategies that are truly transformative. There is so much information included in these chapters; I'll be focusing on helping you learn about interview questions, the keystone pillars you must nail, what types of questions you're likely to be asked, along with a powerful framework that increases your chances of being perceived as a high caliber candidate which obliterates your competition and helps you land the job offer. Let's get started!

Chapter 5: Cracking the Code - Understanding the Three Interview Question Styles

Interviews can feel a bit like walking into the unknown, so in this chapter, I hope to assist you in understanding the types of interview questions you'll likely face. I'll also share the rhyme and reason for using these question types along with your best strategies for answering these styles of questions.

Interview Question Type 1: Situational Questions

Situational questions in interviews pose a hypothetical situation and ask how you would handle the scenario. While these aren't used as commonly, you may still encounter these types of questions.

Example of a situational question:

A team member has consistently missed project deadlines which are now affecting the team's performance. How would you address this situation?

The best way to respond to this question is to pivot into a specific example and describe a time when this happened in the past. I'll show you exactly how to respond and give your answer utilizing my Super STAR Forward methodology in Chapter 9.

Interview Question Type 2: Behavioral-Based Interview Questions

The gold standard for interviews in high performance organizations is behavioral-based questions. These questions focus on your past behavior and experience as indications of how you might handle future workplace challenges. You'll know you're facing a behavioral-based interview question when you hear: "Tell me about a time you..." or "Give me an example of a time when you..."

Example of a behavioral-based interview question:

Tell me about a time when you had to resolve a conflict on your team.

Preparation is the key to answering behavioral-based interview questions. I highly recommend you check out Chapter 7 which covers a multitude of common topics including several behavioral interview questions along with the competencies that the questions are based on. In Chapter 9, I'll teach you about the powerful Super STAR Forward interview answer technique to help you ace these interview questions.

Interview Question Type 3: Simulation Questions

While simulation interview questions aren't commonly used, it's the most effective way to predict on-the-job performance. A simulation-style interview question is used to assess a candidate's ability to apply their real-life experience and knowledge while using their problem-solving skills in a simulated real-world scenario. The goal of the question is to measure how well a candidate can use critical thinking skills to solve problems, adapt to changing conditions, and make decisions under pressure.

Let's demonstrate an example of a simulation-style interview question:

You're a project manager faced with a critical supply shortage just days before a major project deployment. Describe the steps you would take to address this challenge and ensure the project's successful completion.

The best way to answer a simulation question is:

1. Understand the Situation: Get a 360-degree view of the scenario and downstream effects. Ask the interviewer further questions to gain more insight into the situation and parameters.

2. Choose Key Priorities: Prioritize what's most important and urgent and assess the impact of the decisions you're making.

3. Offer Solutions: Summarize the situation and propose the specific steps you would take to solve the issue.

4. Explain Rationale: Explain your reasoning behind the decisions you made. Acknowledge any challenges or risks that may arise from the potential situation and remediation efforts to correct and manage them.

Effectively answering a simulation-style interview question is the single best way to demonstrate your capability to perform the job.

Chapter 6: The Three Job Interview Pillars to Master

Three keystone pillars are the most important factors to having a successful interview that will help you land the job offer. While there are many other aspects to interviewing, as long as you prepare accordingly as covered in Chapter 4, these three pillars will be the most critical elements to landing the job. These three pillars are the Perfect Elevator Pitch, High Performance Interview Answers, and Strategic Interview Closure. When you understand and master these keystone pillars I cover in the next three chapters, you'll dramatically increase your chances of landing the job you desire.

Job Interview Pillars

Pillar 1	Pillar 2	Pillar 3
Perfect Elevator Pitch	High Performance Interview Answers	Strategic Interview Closure

Keystone Pillar 1: The Perfect Elevator Pitch

Imagine stepping into an elevator and finding yourself standing next to your dream employer. You have only 90 seconds to make an unforgettable impression and leave them wanting more. This is where your elevator pitch comes into play.

Your elevator pitch is crucial as it sets the tone for the entire interview. In this chapter, we'll guide you through creating a powerful elevator pitch that disrupts traditional interrogation-style interviews. We'll equip you with the skills to have more conversational interviews that allow your true potential to shine through. Remember, mastering your elevator pitch in 90 seconds will make the rest of the interview feel like a breeze.

Moments matter, especially in interviews. The first ten seconds can make or break your chances. In Chapter 8, I'll share with you, the Perfect Elevator Pitch form - a concise and captivating introduction that highlights your strengths and accomplishments. By crafting an elevator pitch that leaves a powerful impression, you'll grab the interviewer's attention and immediately set yourself apart from the competition.

Keystone Pillar 2: High Performance Interview Answers

I've been in tens of thousands of interviews, and there is a very unique way that the most elusive talent in the world interviews. Less than 1% of all candidates utilize this strategy, and you'll knock the socks off of your interviewer when you start using this keystone pillar during your job interview. In Chapter 9, I'll break down the exact science of responding to interview questions that position you as the best candidate for the job and beat out your competition every time. By understanding and implementing this interview strategy, you'll learn exactly how to showcase your skills, experience, and personality in a way that captivates the interviewer.

Keystone Pillar 3: Strategic Interview Closure

The final keystone pillar is focused on the conclusion of the interview. In Chapter 11, I'll cover the psychological phenomena that are at work and how you can use the end of the interview to subconsciously convince the interviewer that you're the right person for the job and leave a favorable impression.

Chapter 7: Top Interview Questions and Response Strategies

After conducting thousands of interviews, it's safe to say that the questions that may be asked in a job interview can run the gamut. In this chapter, I've gathered the most common types of interview questions you'll be asked. We'll go deeper in Chapter 8 to discuss my methodology for preparing your responses to interview questions.

Below, you'll find two sets of interview questions. The first is a list of general questions that you'll typically face in most standard job interviews. The second list of interview questions below is based on a competency model. These include exceptional work, metrics and analytics, customer focus and experience, problem-solving, ownership, time management, teamwork, learning, alignment and values, communication and style, leadership, influencing skills, and motivation.

It's tempting to try to focus on answering interview questions solely based on successful outcomes, but this can be an indicator of poor performance and a lack of self-awareness. No one is perfect, and interviewers don't expect you to be. I recall one time I asked a candidate about a piece of professional feedback they had received. They responded, "I have never received any negative feedback". Not surprisingly, this candidate was disqualified. Your ability to handle, address, and overcome struggles and challenges is a better indicator of your ability to handle problems on the job and learn from mistakes. Focus on highlighting success and overcoming challenges in your interview answers. It's important to note that interviewers may ask unexpected questions that don't appear on the list below. Using the competency questions below help you prepare your interview answers and allows you to be ready with answers that can be adjusted and applied to a multitude of questions while highlighting your strengths in each of these areas.

Top Interview Questions

Below I have included some of the most frequently asked interview questions used to assess high potential candidates for their experience and qualifications. There are two types of questions to prepare for when beginning to interview with employers: general interview questions and competency category questions. It's worth noting that as you become more senior in your career, these questions will become more job-specific but will still be focused on the same competency areas.

<u>General Questions</u>

1. **Getting to Know You**: In this section, the organization is trying to understand your background and if you are a good match for the company and/or the role.

- Tell me about yourself.

- Why are you interested in this position?

- Why are you interested in this company?

- What do you know about this job?

- What research did you do to be prepared for today?

2. **Work Experience:** An in-depth exploration of your actual work and responsibilities. Interviewers use these questions to determine if your experience is relatable directly or indirectly to the role you are interviewing for.

- Walk me through your experience from the past until the present.

- Why is there a gap in your employment?

- Why did you leave your last job?

3. **Long-Term Viability**: The intention behind these questions is to see if your career path is in line with the organization and if you will be a short-term or long-term employee.

- What are your career aspirations?

- Where do you see yourself in five years?

- What's important to you in your next career move?

Competency Category Questions

For each competency category, prepare two examples for each question: an example of a time when you were successful and a time when you were able to overcome a significant challenge. You do not need to create an answer for each of the questions; try to identify an example that could fit multiple questions under each competency.

1. **Exceptional Work**: Examining your accomplishments helps the interviewer understand the strengths and abilities you bring to the company.

- Tell me about your greatest professional accomplishment.

- Describe a goal that you were able to not only meet but exceed.

2. **Metrics/Analytics**: This is a newer style of question on the interview front. Ultimately, the interviewer wants to know how you have been measured in the past and how you quantitatively impact the business. The more senior the role, the more you should be able to articulate your financial impact on the business.

- Tell me how you have been measured for your performance (or your team's performance) in the past.

- What metrics are you currently (or most recently) using in your role? How are they measured? What have your results been?

3. **Customer Focus**: Customer-centric focus and the ability to handle challenging customers are requirements for every organization.

- Describe a time when you handled an escalated customer or client.

- Tell me about a time when you provided outstanding customer service or client resolution.

4. **Problem-Solving**: This competency is probably one of the most sought-after skills among new employees. The interviewer is seeking to understand if you can be creative in solving complex issues.

- Tell me about a time when you thought outside of the box.

- Tell me about a time when you had to solve a complex problem, only to discover the problem was a symptom of a much larger issue.

5. **Ownership**: A frequently used value for organizations; companies want employees who will take ownership and make sure issues are addressed.

- Tell me about a time you took ownership of a problem or situation without waiting for someone else to resolve it.

- Tell me about a time when you took ownership of a significant project/program that was challenging to implement.

6. **Time Management and Productivity:** The interviewer is assessing your ability to produce work under tight deadlines and hit productivity standards.

- In the past, how have you prioritized your workload?

- What will you do during your first 90 days on the job? *Hint*: This is a simulation question.

7. **Understanding Strengths and Weaknesses**: While this is a very old-school way of assessing your strengths and weaknesses, it still happens. Most candidates do not want to share their weaknesses; this question is asked to evaluate your level of self-awareness. The best way to frame a weakness is to describe how you are improving upon it and any systems or processes you use to mitigate its risk.

- What is your greatest strength? How have you used this strength in previous positions?

- What is your greatest weakness? How have you worked to overcome this challenge?

- What would your last boss say about you?

- Tell me about a professional mistake you've made in the past.

8. **Teamwork**: Being able to work as a part of a team is essential for every organization.

- Tell me about a time when you worked on a team with challenging teammates.

- Discuss a time when you had to earn trust quickly in a professional setting.

9. **Learning**: Continuous learning and improvement are a necessity for today's rapidly changing landscape.

- How do you continue to stay competitive in your field/industry?

- Tell me about a time you had to learn a new skill professionally.

- What is your learning style? How have you used this learning style to increase your skills on the job?

- How do you remain competitive in knowledge and experience in your work or industry?

- What has been the largest learning opportunity you have faced?

10. **Values Alignment:** The interviewer hopes to assess if your values are in alignment with the organization.

- Tell me about a time when your integrity was challenged professionally.

- Describe a time you stood up for something professionally because you didn't feel it was the right thing to do.

11. **Communication**: These questions are used to determine your communication style and aptitude.

- How in the past have you ensured you have communicated effectively with your team?

- Describe a time when there was a miscommunication in the workplace.

12. **Project Management**: Used to assess your ability to manage projects/programs/products while leading team efforts for on-time delivery.

- How have you managed multiple projects and deadlines in the past?

- Describe a time when you took on a challenging project or task.

13. **Leadership and Influence**: These questions are used as an assessment of leadership/management ability and influence.

- Describe a time when you had to influence someone to help you achieve a goal.

- Describe a time when you had to get executive sponsorship for an idea or project that you were working on.

- Describe a time you created a strategy that had a wide organizational impact.

- What is your leadership style? How would you describe your leadership style?

- How do you create buy-in for ideas or projects you are working on? Describe a time in the past.

14. **Motivation**: The interviewer hopes to assess if you are self-motivated or how you can keep your team morale up and motivation in place.

- What would make you lose motivation at work? *Hint*: this can be a tricky question but ultimately nothing should make you lose motivation as you are self-motivated.

- How do you keep your team motivated or engaged in the workplace?

15. **Effectiveness/Efficiency**: Being able to do things bigger, better, and faster, are key indicators of a high potential employee.

- Describe a time when you were able to improve operational efficiency.

- Tell me about a time when you were able to save the company a large amount of money, time, or effort.

- What's the most recent suggestion you made to your employer about improving the workplace?

Chapter 8: The Perfect Elevator Pitch

The single greatest weapon I can help you prepare for in your job search is your elevator pitch. It's the most important moment in your interview and can make or break the interview outcome. In this chapter, I'm going to go deep into creating your Perfect Elevator Pitch; your 90-second career story that captures and communicates your genius, skills, and talents in a way that instantly positions you as top talent and convinces employers that you're the perfect hire for the job.

These days, it's just not enough to be good at your job. You also have to be able to quickly communicate your genius and experience in a way that helps to instantly capture your target audience's attention and sets you apart from the competition. The Perfect Elevator Pitch framework is your chance to highlight your unique value proposition and stand out from other candidates. This 90-second strategy will transform how your interviews go from this point forward. During job interviews, the prompt 'Tell me about yourself' is often used as an icebreaker to kick off the conversation.When you hear this question, I want you to recognize this opening volley as a cue that this is the time to use your elevator pitch. I want you to be best prepared for your interview by creating your Perfect Elevator Pitch using the framework below and having it ready to use at your disposal. Rarely is a candidate prepared to answer this question effectively and powerfully. You'll be astounded by how differently people treat you when you answer this softball question with a powerful statement that instantly anchors you in your position as top talent.

The Perfect Elevator Pitch Formula

"I AM" Statement $+$ Career Journey Story $+$ Future Vision $=$ Perfect Elevator Pitch

Let's break down the 3 key ingredients to assembling your Perfect Elevator Pitch:

Step 1 - Present: Your "I AM" Statement

First impressions are the most impactful in an interview. The first moments when you meet any new person are the most important; research has shown that within the first 30 seconds we cement the impression of who we are from the other person's perspective (Renner, 2018). It's also during this time that we have the opportunity to use anchor bias to our advantage as this first impression will follow us through the interview process (Furnham & Boo, 2011). To use this to our advantage in an interview, we need to nail the first part of our elevator pitch: the "I AM" Statement.

Frame Disruption Technique

One powerful technique to cement your expertise and authority is to use frame disruption. This concept was introduced in the book "Pitch Anything," and we will use this concept to disrupt the usual interview dynamics. By utilizing frame disruption, you can reset the expectations of the interviewer and position yourself in a high power position.

That means the first words out of our mouth in the interview need to begin with your "I AM" statement. This is the present version of who you are professionally. It's really common that people want to go straight into describing their past when answering this question, but that anchors in a past version of who you are. Tell your interviewer who you are today, because that's the person they are interviewing.

Think about answering the "I AM" Statement in this mad libs fill-in-the-blank format:

I am a \<adjective #1\> and \<adjective #2\> \<level of professional\> with more than \<# of years experience\> in \<verb\> \<powerful result\> for \<types of companies, industries, clients, or users you specialize in\>.

Let me give you an example of what this statement would look like for a Senior Leader in Human Resources:

Example: I am a passionate and ambitious Human Resources executive with more than 19 years of experience in talent management, driving powerful human capital strategy results for Fortune 100 high-tech organizations like Google, Facebook, and Amazon.

Get Strategic & Specific

Now the next stage of building your present state is to add two specific examples of your work history that demonstrate what you've just declared in your "I AM" statement.

Here's an example for our Senior Human Resources Leader:

Example 1: At Google, I created a new talent acquisition strategy that cut the organization's time-to-fill by 32% and raised the quality of hire by 22%. By focusing on innovating sourcing strategies and streamlining hiring processes, I was able to cut time-to-fill from 60 to 42 days, securing top talent for growth.

Example 2: At Facebook, I drove retention strategy and decreased the turnover rate by 15% in 2 years. This was achieved with personalized career paths and career design workshops which increased retention and also achieved a 25% increase in internal promotions via mentorship and individualized learning initiatives.

These specific examples immediately cement our position as who we declared ourselves to be in the first 'I AM' statement. The next question that inevitably pops into your interviewer's head will be, 'How did you get to that place in your career?' We immediately answer this question for them by heading into Step 2, which is focused on your past and describing your career journey.

Step 2 - Past: Describe Your Career Journey Story

Once we declare our present state, the next step is to focus on describing the journey that led us to who we are today. It's common for people to put their past first, but anchor bias locks in the perception of who we are by what we say first (Furnham & Boo, 2011). Therefore, the present must come first and the past second. Use Step 2 to describe your career path to highlight where you started in your field and the projects and/or promotions that prepared you for your next career move.

Here's an example of the past career journey of our Senior Human Resources Leader:

Example: I started my professional journey as a HR specialist at Amazon, where I honed my skills in employee development and engagement. As I took on more responsibilities and guided teams through intricate human capital projects, I transitioned into a human resources leadership role overseeing organizational growth strategies. This hands-on experience led to my leadership role at Facebook where I focused on talent management and crafted innovative talent acquisition methods that focused on key metrics for increasing retention and internal promotions. From there, I was recruited to an executive talent management role at Google where I focused on aligning company objectives with headcount growth and employee engagement.

The next step is about the future, where we paint a picture of what we desire in our next career move.

Step 3 - Future: Paint the Future Vision

One of the standard interview questions you'll be asked is 'What do you want to be doing next in your career?' or even 'Why are you interested in this role?' We can proactively answer these questions and also communicate what an employer would need to offer for us to consider a career opportunity. I've personally seen my clients' results from this specific step inspire an interviewer to shift and change the job title and description to meet the needs of a candidate. Remember, that when you're considered top talent, everything is negotiable and employers will go above and beyond to bring a superstar hire onto their team. In your future statement, I want you to emphasize what you want and not what you bring to the table as we covered in Steps 1 and 2. Focus on what you desire in your next career, what level of position and influence you want, what type of organization you want to work with, and even initiatives and projects you would like to lead. The key part of this is tying it all together; matching what you desire together and what the company is hiring for. If you can communicate a desire that happens to align your background and desired career path exactly with what the company is looking for, you'll immediately be seen as the most highly desirable candidate.

Here's an example of the future state desires for our Senior Human Resources Leader:

Example: In my next career opportunity, I am looking to take on an executive HR leadership role inside a rapidly growing technology startup that is redefining its industry landscape. I am excited to lead a dynamic and employee-centric HR team in crafting innovative human capital strategies that help increase employee engagement while also aligning seamlessly with the company's aggressive revenue targets and consumer growth goals. Next, we'll put all three steps together to create the Perfect Elevator Pitch.

Step 4: Put it All Together

The last step is to combine your present, past, and future into one single elevator pitch that can be communicated to your interviewer(s) in under 90 seconds. Using the Senior HR leader's examples above, here's this candidate's Perfect Elevator Pitch.

An Example of the Perfect Elevator Pitch

"I AM" Statement: I am a passionate and ambitious Human Resources executive with more than 19 years of experience in talent management, driving powerful human capital strategy results for Fortune 100 high-tech organizations like Google, Facebook, and Amazon. At Google, I created a new talent acquisition strategy that cut the organization's time-to-fill by 32% and raised the quality of hire by 22%. By focusing on innovating sourcing strategies and streamlining hiring processes, I was able to cut time-to-fill from 60 to 42 days, securing top talent for growth. At Facebook, I drove retention strategy and decreased the turnover rate by 15% in 2 years. This was achieved with personalized career paths and career design workshops which increased retention and also achieved a 25% increase in internal promotions via mentorship and individualized learning initiatives.

Career Journey Story: I started my professional journey as a HR specialist at Amazon, where I honed my skills in employee development and engagement. As I took on more responsibilities and guided teams through intricate human capital projects, I transitioned into a human resources leadership role overseeing organizational growth strategies. This hands-on experience led to my leadership role at Facebook where I focused on talent management, and crafted innovative talent acquisition methods that focused on key metrics for increasing retention and internal promotions. From there, I was recruited to an executive talent management role at Google where I focused on aligning company objectives with headcount growth and employee engagement.

Future Vision: In my next career opportunity, I am looking to take on an executive HR leadership role inside of a rapidly growing technology startup that is redefining its industry landscape. I am excited to lead a dynamic and employee-centric HR team in crafting innovative human capital strategies that help increase employee engagement while also aligning seamlessly with the company's aggressive revenue targets and consumer growth goals.

I hope you can see how different this strategy is from most of the advice out there in the marketplace. This seamless transition between the candidate's present state, work history, and career objectives combines the approach of frame disruption, strategically communicating their value, and declaring what they want next in their career. I hope you can imagine just how powerful this approach is at disrupting the interviewer's expectations and how it immediately increases your power position and denotes you as top talent. Now this text may look like a mouthful, but I used a stopwatch while I recited it myself and it clocks in at a near-perfect 91 seconds. It doesn't take a long time to make a powerful first impression. Your next action is to craft your own Perfect Elevator Pitch using the framework above. When you're finished, congratulate yourself and then head on to Chapter 9: High Performance Interview Answers.

Chapter 9:
High Performance
Interview Answers

N ow that we've covered the most common interview questions, let's talk about how to answer them. The quality of your interview questions will determine the quality of your interview outcomes. The bottom line is, you've got to nail your interview answers if you want to land a job offer. Below, I'm going to first cover how to convey your resume experience. The "walk me through your resume" interview question is a landmine for many candidates who are anxious that interviewers will discover gaps and unsavory reasons for them. Trust that if you follow my direction, you'll be able to maintain your power position and effectively communicate your value even if you have had a break in your employment history. Next, I'll cover my Super STAR Forward methodology for answering behavioral interview questions in a way that will make you the top 1%

of all candidates. This is your secret weapon to blowing your competition out of the water and having companies bang down your door with job offers.

Describing Your Career Journey

Inevitably, you'll be reviewing your resume with an interviewer. You'll likely be asked to share your career journey dozens of times on the path to your next job offer. It's important to recognize that while your resume gets you in the door, that's about all it does. The rest relies upon you to show up and dig deeper to explain your experience and accomplishments. When a recruiter or interviewer asks you to 'walk me through your resume,' follow these guidelines:

- Always review your resume with your interviewer from the most recent and work your way backwards from present to the past.

- When sharing a specific position, start by saying 'At (company name), I held the position of (title) where I was responsible for (short synopsis of your role).' Keep this short and brief and increase your perceived authority by discussing the size of the department, team, project(s), and/or P&L you were responsible for.

- Immediately go into your accomplishments demonstrating impact and scope at the company. These are not the same as your responsibilities and many people focus on tasks and job description duties thinking they are the most important part of their resume. Instead focus on what results and accomplishments you achieved at a company and how that impacted the team, project, and/or bottom line. You will get hired for what you accomplish, not for the tasks you completed from your job description.

- Don't volunteer your reason for leaving any job. You can transition any career movement from one job to another by saying, "I then accepted an opportunity with (company name)" or "I was offered an opportunity at (company name)" and then continue reviewing your resume, highlighting your accomplishments, impact, and scope of work. There's no need to mention whether you were terminated or laid off from a previous employer unless directly asked. Avoid using the terminology "let go" in all cases.

- Don't volunteer explanations for gaps. Candidates get really concerned that a recruiter will spot a gap and dig in for details. Rest assured, any experienced recruiter has seen huge gaps on well-qualified candidates' resumes. What matters to a recruiter when they see a gap is that you can convey you are still able to successfully compete against others in the marketplace for your role or industry. Gaps are very common for highly talented candidates, especially after the Great Recession and the pandemic. Candidates tend to make a bigger deal of gaps than the interviewer does. I like to say that the only time you should be concerned enough to create a detailed explanation for a gap is if it is longer than six months. My favorite verbiage for explaining gaps is to let the recruiter or interviewer know that you've 'had the luxury of taking some time to focus on (insert personal/professional development pursuit) while deciding what career opportunities to explore further.' This language pattern is one of detachment and shows the recruiter that you're not desperate, that you are weighing your many job opportunities at hand, and that you're looking for the right move in your career journey, not just any job. This positioning is a trait of top talent and increases your power position.

Following these guidelines allows you to tell your career journey story from a position of power and detachment while showcasing the scope of your impact during your employment, which will help increase your perception of being a top candidate for the job.

Using the STAR Technique to Respond to Interview Questions

The hardest part of any interview is providing the interviewer with impressive examples that indicate the level of your expertise and experience. One of the most common techniques I found myself needing to teach new recruiters is how to skillfully probe to help a candidate respond with a specific example. This challenge is precisely what the original STAR technique was created for; it was designed to help candidates establish a specific framework for how to respond to questions. Providing concrete examples of your past accomplishments when responding to behavioral-based questions is the most effective way to showcase the quality of your candidacy. Most candidates are familiar with the STAR technique for responding to interview questions.

The acronym STAR stands for:

S/T: Situation or Task
A: Action
R: Result

Truth be told, most candidates do not do a great job of responding in a STAR format. Many times, they focus on the situation and action, and fail to share any result. This is a problem because the result is what gets you the job. Always focus on showing the impact of your action to create a result for the organization. Once you've understood the power of showcasing your impact, it's time to get deeper into the evolution of the STAR philosophy.

The Super STAR Forward Methodology

The top 1% of all candidates have unknowingly mastered a concept that I have discovered during my two decades in corporate recruiting. They took the STAR interview technique and added their own unique spin to it. After studying these interview answers for over a decade, I concluded that the top candidates sandwiched their STAR examples with even more powerful stories that amplified the value of their candidacy. I saw firsthand how hiring managers would compete internally for these candidates because they were so impressive. I'll show you this groundbreaking technique that will take you from the average candidate in the process to an absolute superstar.

Introducing the Super STAR Forward Methodology:

Super STAR Forward Methodology

| Super (Strategic) |
| Situation/Task |
| Action |
| Result |
| Forward Looking |

Let's begin by breaking down each piece of the formula.

Super: Strategic - The super part of this interview answer is the strategic layer of the example. It's just not enough to jump right in and talk about what happened. You need to go beyond that and explain why the situation you dealt with is important and impacts the overall organization and/or team.

S/T: Situation/Task - Like the original, the next three steps are the same. The S/T is focused on describing the situation. Paint a vivid picture of the situation and the challenge you faced. The best scenarios to share are where you saved the organization money while also serving the customer as this demonstrates your ability to balance the company's bottom line while ensuring client satisfaction.

A: Action - In this step, focus on sharing the real-life actions you took to mediate and resolve the situation.

R: Result - The most important part of the answer is the result. Be clear about what happened and focus on quantifying the result of your action. Specific metrics that include analytics, percentages, ROI, or bottom-line impacts are particularly powerful.

Forward: Forward-Looking Vision - The absolute clincher in this interview answer is to go deeper into the result. Evaluate how you ensured that this situation 'always or never' happened again with a forward-looking vision. This shows a strategic level of insight that is focused on continuous process improvement. You'll knock your interviewer's socks off when you add this element to your answers.

Mastering the Super STAR Forward Answer

Now that you know the fundamentals of the formula, let's compare a STAR answer with a Super STAR Forward answer to contrast the difference. Let's assume the candidate is interviewing for a senior customer service position at a contact center and is well qualified having spent the last two years working in a call center environment.

Interview Question: Describe a time you dealt with an agitated customer and how you handled it.

STAR Answer

Situation/Task: A customer called in and was irate and upset about their billing statement. This was the second time that she had contacted the call center and stated that she wanted to end her services with us.

Action: I began by apologizing for the situation and then investigated the customer's billing. I found that we had incorrectly billed the customer over the last 3 months. I immediately corrected the customer's account and as part of our customer retention strategy, I offered her a free month of service.

Result: The customer was so relieved to have this resolved during a positive interaction with our call center. She thanked me for my help and decided to stay with our service. She was so impressed that she wrote a kudos letter to my supervisor.

Super STAR Forward Answer

Super (Strategic): A goal for our call center in Q3 was to achieve a 94% customer retention rate. This situation happened at the end of the last month of the quarter and the team was at a 93% rating. This meant that every call that came in had the opportunity to make or break it for achieving our overall goal.

Situation/Task: A customer called in and was irate and upset about their billing statement. This was the second time that she had contacted the call center and stated that she wanted to end her services with us.

Action: I began by apologizing for the situation and then investigated the customer's billing. I found that we had incorrectly billed the customer over the last 3 months. I immediately corrected the customer's account and as part of our customer retention strategy, I offered her a free month of service.

Result: The customer was so relieved to have this resolved during a positive interaction with our call center. She thanked me for my help and decided to stay with our service. She was so impressed that she wrote a kudos letter to my supervisor.

Forward Looking: I realized that the billing error that had occurred was the second time that week I had encountered it. I decided to investigate further and realized we had a surcharge that was being billed to the wrong accounts. I brought this to my supervisor, and we were able to identify 103 accounts that had contacted us recently that had incorrect billing and wanted to cancel their services. We created a plan to reach out to each of these customers, address the situation, and offer a resolution. We were able to retain 67 accounts which helped us to achieve our customer retention goal for the quarter.

After this call, I then set up a reminder on my calendar to check in with the customer's account the next month. When I did, I saw that the account billing remained accurate and sent a secure message to follow-up with the customer to let her know that I was checking in based on our last conversation and that everything looked okay on her account, and asked her to reach out to me if she needed anything more. She remained a happy customer throughout the rest of my time in that position.

Compare these two answers and answer this: Who would you want to hire? If you said the Super STAR Forward, you'd be right. It's time to take your interview responses to the next level. When my clients use this technique, they blow away their competition. Many times, it has created a sense of urgency that makes the hiring manager offer them the job the same day they are interviewed. This technique is an absolute game changer in the world of interviews and helps you stand out as a truly exceptional candidate.

A Super STAR Forward Answer follows the well-known STAR (Situation/Task, Action, Result) method, but with a strategic twist. By adding the Super (strategic) layer and Forward (forward-looking vision) to your responses, you will prove yourself as a strategic high caliber candidate who not only solves present challenges but also creates processes or strategies to prevent future issues.

Chapter 10: The Altruism Advantage

"*Those who help others without the expectation of any-thing in return directly increase the quality of their own lives.*" — *Lindsay Mustain*

This quote is a powerful statement that blew my mind when I found that science backed up my core belief, especially when it came to job searching. Research has shown that happier people perform more acts of kindness. What's remarkable is that performing a kind act toward others increases our own happiness (Otake et al., 2006). Let's take the concept of connecting altruism to happiness a little further. People who are happier rate higher levels of well-being (Lyubomirsky et al., 2005).

What was found was that individuals with reported higher levels of well-being received a multitude of benefits:

- More positive experiences in life

- Better interpersonal relationships

- Reported being healthier than their peers

- Experienced improved mental health

What's even more incredible is how the study identified that well-being impacts occupational happiness, employment status, and income (Otake et al., 2006). People who report higher levels of well-being were found to:

- Be less likely to lose their jobs

- More likely to receive a call back for further interviews in the hiring process

- Hold positions that offer more autonomy and variety

- Perform meaningful work at their organization

- Even when study subjects were unemployed, participants were more likely to be reemployed by the study follow-up period than their peers

- Measured over a five-year period of time, individuals reporting higher well-being saw an increased income level

That's a huge testament to the power of using the Altruism Advantage, and I want to invite you to use it for your job search.

Would you lend a hand to someone you don't know with zero expectations of being recognized or rewarded for it? If you immediately said yes, then you're definitely my type of person. I have a humble request from someone you've never met who could use your assistance right now. This person is like a former version of you - stuck in their job search, feeling scared and lost, and doing their best to improve their odds of landing a job. So here's my request. When I sat down, I wrote this book for that individual, who just like Daphne in the introduction, is feeling broken down by the job search process. For me to reach my goal of getting this book into the hands of the people I created it for, it depends on word of mouth. Your honest feedback can help bring this book to the attention of someone job searching and assist them with the guidance they need in their job search. If you've found insights in this book that will improve your job search outcomes, would you please take a few minutes to share your thoughts by leaving a review?

By investing less than a minute in sharing your feedback, you can:

- Assist one more job seeker in finding their path

- Guide one more individual toward meaningful work

- Help close the gap for one person to finally land a job offer

- Help a family that is struggling because of unemployment

- Make someone's life a little more hopeful and better

If you're on board with helping, here's all you need to do (and it should take you less than sixty seconds):

- If you're physically reading this book - head to Amazon, and choose a star rating and leave a quick review with a few sentences about what you learned or enjoyed

- If you're listening on Audible - head to the end of the book and you'll automatically be prompted to leave a rating and a review

- If you're reading on an e-reader/kindle or the Kindle

app - scroll to the end and you should see a request for a review pop up

- Should you be on a different platform than the above, a review on the Amazon book page goes a long way to increasing the visibility of this book and helps others find it when they're frustrated while job searching

A rising tide lifts all boats and this principle holds true now. By sharing your insights, you've now contributed to a network of support that benefits us all. Your desire to help another person you've never met who is in a difficult circumstance truly touches my heart. I'm so grateful to share the insider tips and strategies inside this book with you. When we share value with others, it's an easy way to increase our connection with one another and we associate higher perceived value with that individual. This means if you introduce something impactful to someone else's life, they'll associate you with that value. If you feel inclined, pass this book along to another job seeker and reap the Altruism Advantage. My deepest thanks for spending time to help spread the word about this book; it truly means the world to me. Let's move on to the final Milestone which is all about closing the deal and securing the job offer.

Milestone V: Closing the Deal - Elevating Your Interview to Offer

Andrew had been job searching for nine months after being laid off from his supply chain job. The situation had gotten so dire that he had taken a job stocking shelves at the local big box store, at minimum wage, just to keep food on the table for his family. He contacted me when a huge retailer requested an interview with him after seeing his logistics experience. After having so many job interviews go south, he told me, 'I've got to win this one, Lindsay.' We focused on all aspects of the interview prep, especially finishing the interview strong. The end of the interview process is where you can directly cement your position as the top candidate and leave a lasting impression that turns an interview into a job offer. After his interview, he let me know, 'I followed everything you said. The recruiter just called to let me know that they want to extend a job offer.' The advertised salary started at $80K annually, but we were able to negotiate up to $98K and get a relocation package. The next message that came from Andrew reminded me why I do what I do: "Thank you soooooo much for everything, Lindsay. It is just words but I cannot express the feelings. I am so excited to begin the next chapter of my life."

Once you've reached Milestone V of the interview process, you've made it to the final stage of effective interviewing. Inside this milestone, I'm going to be sharing with you how to finish your interview strong by utilizing the end of the interview and follow-up process to emphasize your strengths and cement your position as a top candidate. The interview process is driven by humans and therefore inherently flawed by design. There are ways that you can position yourself to come out ahead of the competition by using some psychological insights that will leave a lasting impression on the interviewer while increasing your chances of receiving a job offer.

These closure strategies extend beyond the interview room, and to finish strong, a follow-up strategy needs to be followed. The way you end the interview has the advantage of coloring the entire interview as positive or negative while ensuring you'll get a call back from the recruiter. In a world filled with ghosting and waiting, this is a true game changer that will help you land a job offer more quickly.

The final chapter of this milestone will recap of the biggest pitfalls that can happen to even the most qualified candidates. Be sure that as you navigate through the interview, you avoid these pitfalls or risk losing the job opportunity.

This milestone is where we bring it all together. The Ace Your Interview system combines strategic thinking, and knowledge of industry best practices, along with the process to stand out among other candidates, to help you secure your dream career opportunity.

Chapter 11: Strategic Interview Closure - Leaving a Lasting Impression

The final keystone pillar is how you end the interview. The reason is that there is a combination of psychological phenomena that are happening at this moment that can be used to your advantage. The first one is called the horn or halo effect. The horn or halo effect is a bias where the interviewer may perceive the interview as highly qualified or not qualified in one desired area and then rate it correspondingly high or low across the board (Noor et al., 2023).

The second phenomenon is called the recency bias. When this bias is happening, it means the interviewer may overemphasize the most recent experience with the candidate when we consider how things will go in the future (Recency Effect

- an Overview | ScienceDirect Topics, n.d.). So why does this matter? It means you need to be strategic in how you end your interview. Our goal in the Strategic Interview Closure step is to close out strongly to give you a halo effect and positive recency bias. We do this through a process that I call The Resell.

The Resell

At the end of each interview, most interviewers allow time to ask you if you have any questions. Most candidates jump right into tactical questions that do not help the interviewer see you as the ideal candidate. The Resell is a strategy we use at the end of the interview to utilize the questions that we ask at the end to overcome the interviewers' objections and 'resell' ourselves as the candidate of choice to help us land the job offer. The Resell strategy is composed of asking four questions of the interviewer. If you are actively inside of an interview loop with other interviews scheduled, you should only ask the timing question once and preferably to the hiring manager or most senior member of the interview loop. Below, you'll find the style of questions to ask and the goal behind each of the questions.

Questions #1 and #2: Strategic Questions

The goal of the first two questions is to focus on asking a strategic question that demonstrates that you are a top candidate and able to solve a company's challenges. The secret to creating a strategic question is to ask about how the next hire can support a company or team goal with a specific timeline. Prepare these first two questions ahead of time and bring them to the interview.

Here are some examples of a strategic style question:

1. What goals/objectives is your team currently working on to achieve by the end of the year (or next quarter)?

2. What are some of the challenges your department/team is facing in (insert current year)?

3. What are some of the core objectives this person will need to address in the first 90 days?

4. What do the internal or external customers need from this person that will fill the job during the first 30 days?

The key part of using strategic questions is not in just getting the answer to the question, but in using the responses to affirm their answer and share an example of a time when you have handled a similar situation. This is where you resell your candidacy to the interviewer and show that you are capable, qualified, and ready to achieve their strategic goals.

Question #3: Passion Point Question

You must build rapport and establish a genuine connection with your interviewer(s). People like what is like them and we use this when crafting our third question. This third question is meant to tap into the passions and desires the interviewer has and to showcase that you care about and can support those goals as well. This question cannot be preplanned as each interviewer is different, so you'll want to take notes on what points the interviewer brings up during the interview that you may emphasize when asking the third question.

Here are some examples of creating a passion point question:

1. The interviewer expressed concern about the future of revenue growth in their organization. You could ask a question about what they've personally identified as key ways to grow revenue for their team/department or in the fiscal year.

2. The interviewer showed a passion for situational leadership. You could ask how they've used situational leadership in the development of their team members.

By demonstrating a shared passion and commitment to similar affinities, you'll be able to forge a deeper connection with the interviewer that will set you apart from other candidates.

Question #4: Confirm the Timeline

This question is asked only once during the interview (or interview loop if interviews happen with multiple interviewers). It is a question of timing and about the next steps in the process. This question is imperative to allow us to understand when we should hear back and an appropriate timeline for follow-up.

Here are some examples of timeline questions:

1. What do the next steps look like?

2. When can I expect to hear back about the next step?

Please note: Be sure to confirm a specific date or volunteer one (e.g. should I expect to hear back by next Friday?) and let them agree or give you a date. You need to have a timeline established to be able to follow-up appropriately. If the interviewer or hiring manager won't confirm timing, take that as a lack of interest or they may be lacking aptitude for effective hiring. You can also let the potential employer know that at this point you have many opportunities that you are being considered for (if accurate), so you want to know the timing in case you're offered another opportunity since you're very interested in the role/company you just interviewed with or for.

Thanking the Interviewer

After you've asked your questions and the interview is conducted, use this terminology with your interviewer. "(Interviewer Name), it's been a pleasure to meet you and I appreciate your time today. It would be an honor to have the opportunity to work with you." Use this phrase no matter how well or poorly the interview has gone. Recency bias says that the most recent interaction clouds our perception of events, so even if your interview has not gone well, this lets you end on a positive note that may increase your chances of moving forward to the next step of the interview process.

Chapter 12: Navigating and Overcoming Common Interview Pitfalls

If you're looking to impress your future employer, it's a combination of what to do and what not to do. In this chapter, I'm going to be sharing with you some of the common pitfalls that candidates face. Some of these will be obvious, but after hiring 10,343 people, I've found that common sense isn't too common when it comes to searching for a job.

Pitfall #1: Being Late or No Showing

Show up for in-person interviews fifteen minutes early (no more or less). Log on to video interviews five minutes before your call starts. Always let an interviewer know if you are unable to attend the interview; this is a basic courtesy and will likely get you blacklisted from a company in the future if you don't give them notice.

Pitfall #2: Not Being Specific In Your Interview Answers

This is the single greatest problem in the thousands of interviews I've conducted in my career. Be specific when answering the questions from your interviewer. Chapter 9 covers the Super STAR Forward methodology to follow for the ideal interview answer.

Pitfall #3: Not Building Rapport

Rapport builds familiarity and trust. We hire people we trust to do the job well. Following the strategies I've included throughout this book will help you to build rapport with your interviewers. You can also build rapport by smiling, being warm in your responses, showing interest and empathy, finding common ground, and using the interviewer's name.

Pitfall #4: Interrupting the Interviewer

Let the interviewer speak, even if you are in the middle of a thought. Interruptions are usually because an interviewer wants to know more about what you are sharing. This is a good thing because it shows they are interested, listening, and engaged in what you are saying. To be sure I have continuity in my interview answers, I always recommend you take note of where you stopped so you can seamlessly pick up where you left off.

Pitfall #5: Talking Too Fast

It's common to speak quickly in an interview because nerves have gotten the best of you. Be sure to slow your pace down to model and match the pace of the interviewer. I cover this in detail in Chapter 4.

Pitfall #6: Talking For Too Long

Being verbose in an interview is a common reason candidates get rejected from the process. There is limited time in the interview and you want to allow the interviewer the chance to ask all of their questions. Focus on responding to the interview question in less than three minutes to allow time for follow-up questions. Be concise and know your audience.

Pitfall #7: Not Allowing Silence

There are always going to be questions that stump you in an interview. If this happens, it's best to pause and think about this interview question. If it takes more than a few moments, you can say to the interviewer "Is it okay to let me think about this for just a moment?" An experienced interviewer understands that silence is normal in the interview process. If you're struggling to come up with a situation, don't say "I don't know." Instead, say "I've got a situation that is similar but may not be exactly what you're looking for. Is it okay if I share this with you and you can let me know if you would like me to share another example?" This allows you to answer the question while giving the interviewer the insight that they can ask for a follow-up example if it doesn't meet what they're looking for.

Pitfall #8: Answering Interview Questions Incorrectly

Interviewers will sometimes ask unclear questions and you may be unsure of what they're asking. If this happens to you, feel free to ask the interviewer to repeat the question. If you're still uncertain, paraphrase the question and ask the interviewer if this is what they were asking for. This should allow you to provide the appropriate answer to the question.

If you fail to answer an interview question correctly because you misheard or misunderstood it, you'll want to take steps quickly to correct that action. Be sure that you're keeping a close eye on how your interviewer responds to your answers. If they react surprised or uncertain, you can tell me "I'm sorry if I misunderstood the question or that wasn't the type of example you were looking for. Could you share the question again and I'll be happy to provide an answer that's closer to what you hoped to learn?" This phrase allows you to get a second chance at answering the question. You should never say, "I don't know" in an interview. This phrase is the fastest way to be rejected from a job opportunity.

Pitfall #9: Acting Like a Tell-All Book

The interview is a place to show your highlight reel; it's not your confessional. Don't volunteer negative things about yourself. I cover how to address challenging situations on your resume in Chapter 9. Always focus on showing your best side to the interviewer.

Pitfall #10: Being Negative

Avoid speaking poorly about your previous employer or former teammates; speaking disparagingly about anything in the interview is a red flag for an employer. Sometimes, our previous employer left a bad taste in our mouths, but there is always something to be grateful for even if it is only that they paid you to be there or filled in some space on your resume. Always find the positive.

Pitfall #11: Being Rude or Unkind

Your interview is all about making the best impression. I guarantee that if you're rude to the receptionist, the interviewer will hear about it. Be kind to every person from the moment you walk out your door as you never know who you will encounter on your way to your interview. Be a class act, always.

Pitfall #12: Using Your Phone Inappropriately

When you show up for your interview, stay present and focused on the situation. Don't talk on your phone or play games. Make sure your phone is set to silent. Take a look around the waiting area for company materials to review and be engaged which will help you put your best foot forward.

Pitfall #13: Not Being Presentable

If you come to an interview looking like you just rolled out of bed and haven't showered in a week, your interview will probably be over before it even starts. This is the time to make sure you are presentable and showcasing what you bring to the job.

Pitfall #14: Poor Body Language

I once interviewed a candidate who had their arms behind their head rocking in their chair for the entire duration of the interview. If you are slumped over in your chair with crossed arms and a poor expression on your face, you're not likely to make a great impression. Be aware that your body language communicates more than the words you speak. In Chapter 4, I cover ways to strategically use body language in your interview.

Pitfall #15: Not Being Prepared

Lack of preparation will penalize you in an interview:

- Be fully prepared for an interview. This book shows you exactly how to create an elevator pitch, respond to interview questions, and end the interview. Prepare and practice each of those keystone pillars in Chapter 6.

- Dress neatly and appropriately for the interview, from head to toe, and bring a padfolio with you.

- Bring five copies of your resume with you when you're interviewing in person. If you don't have a printer, head to your local office supply store to have them printed.

- Bring water and a snack if you have a full day of interviews to keep you hydrated and energized for the day.

Video interviews have an added degree of preparation required.

- Make sure your background is clean and quiet. Ensure your environment is, and will remain, distraction and interruption free.

- Focus on good eye contact. Simulate eye contact on video by looking directly below the camera rather than at the computer screen. Eye contact builds rapport and trust with your interviewer.

- Make sure you have tested and ensured your technology and internet are working before the interview begins. Log on five minutes early to start your interview promptly.

Pitfall #16: Not Asking Questions

The end of the interview is the perfect opportunity to help cement you as the candidate of choice for this position. Chapter 11 gives you the perfect playbook for planning your end-of-interview questions and strategically closing out the interview to leave the best impression.

Pitfall #17: Asking For Feedback In the Interview

I don't know who is giving this advice, but please avoid it at all costs. When a candidate asks "How did I do?" or "Are there any objections to my candidacy?", it indicates they're asking for validation. Validation-seeking behavior is seen as neediness, a low value candidate tactic that repels your dream employers. I understand the desire to receive feedback and ask for a chance to overcome objections; this is not the best way to achieve these goals. Avoid asking this type of question and focus on the strategic approach I discuss in Chapter 6, with the three interview keystone pillars. Using this strategy comes from a place of power rather than neediness.

Pitfall #18: Getting Impatient

Being calm and patient in the process will aid you much more than being impatient with your interviewer. Be prepared to be asked the same questions over and over again and for delays in the hiring process. Most of the time, this behavior from candidates comes from feeling pressure to land a job quickly. Please be patient with your recruiter and hiring manager, and know when to move on if you're being ghosted in the process. The best way to decrease the stakes and pressure of a single job interview is to create leverage in your job search. At the end of Chapter 2, I discuss how to create leverage as a high caliber candidate.

Pitfall #19: Not Following Up

They say the fortune is in the follow-up so make this a standard practice for your interviews. You should always close out an interview by asking for the timeline (Chapter 11). Always send your interviewer a thank you note via email; it's even better if you can send them a physical note. If your recruiter/hiring manager has not reached out to you by the timeline they gave in the interview, you should follow the post-interview follow-up strategy as covered in Chapter 12.

Pitfall #20: Following Up Aggressively

Do not stalk your recruiter. I have had candidates call me 20 times in a row during the time I was on a 30-minute phone interview. Following up aggressively is inappropriate for a professional environment and indicates that you're likely to be a challenging employee. Go back to Pitfall #18 to remember how to conduct yourself appropriately.

Pitfall #21: Not Being Timely in Responding

Keep an eye on your email and phone when job searching and respond the same day to any interview inquiries (don't forget to check your junk mailbox). The reason you should respond quickly is based on my personal experience of hiring thousands of candidates. The candidates who are consistently rated the highest against their peers are also the quickest to respond to job postings and interview requests.

Conclusion

You made it! I want to first thank you for diving deep into this topic and letting me share the transformational impact of the Ace Your Interview System. The strategic approach of an effective interview will allow you to see massive results in your job search. Throughout this book, I've focused on giving you strategic perspectives from a Fortune 500 recruiter and career coach. Let's revisit the core insights we've covered along the way:

- **Master Your Mindset.** Here's your reminder that 80% of the job search game comes down to getting in the right headspace throughout the interview process. Remember, you are a valuable employee and any employer will be lucky to have you on their team.

- **Get Specific.** Don't be afraid to step into your power. Own your results and express pride in your work and the impact it has had on previous organizations.

- **Tell Your Story.** Your stories highlighting your unique abilities are the key to your power in the interview process. Share your Super STAR Forward examples with pride at the highest level and watch how your interview results increase.

- **Dig Deep.** Be proud to showcase your accomplishments. Don't shy away from sharing the impact and scope you've had in the past so interviewers can easily see what you'll do the same at the next company.

- **Use the Power of Psychology.** With over 100 human biases at work in decision-making, let's use these to strengthen our position. Start and end the interview strongly to get the best results.

- **Seal the Deal.** There is power in closing strong and an effective follow-up strategy. Your ability to cultivate multiple opportunities for your next career move will directly impact the leverage you have in these follow-up conversations.

- **Focus on Continuous Improvement.** The further along in your career, the more powerful the strategies I've shared within these pages. Hone your interviewing aptitude with the Ace the Interview System and it will change the trajectory of your career journey.

You're prepared for the journey ahead. I am proud of the commitment, dedication, and work that you have put in, and I know you will continue to do so to improve your career ascension.

An Invitation:

If you're wondering what's next, keep reading. The path I've shared in this book is not for everyone—it's for those ready to embrace their potential and ascend their career through the process of Intentional Career Design. If you're ready to rapidly uplevel your career, beat out the competition, do work that matters, and earn the best salary of your life, I invite you to apply to work with me directly.

Head to **intentionalcareerdesign.com** to embark on the transformative career journey that awaits. The next chapter of your career is yours to write - let's craft it together.

References

1. Cuddy, A. (2012, June). Your body language may shape who you are. Ted.com; TED Talks. https://www.ted.com/talks/amy_cuddy_your_body_language_may_shape_who_you_are

2. Furnham, A., & Boo, H. C. (2011). A literature review of the anchoring effect. The Journal of Socio-Economics, 40(1), 35–42. https://doi.org/10.1016/j.soc ec.2010.10.008

3. Lyubomirsky, S., King, L., & Diener, E. (2005). The Benefits of Frequent Positive Affect: Does Happiness Lead to Success? Psychological Bulletin, 131(6), 803–855. https://doi.org/10.1037/0033-2909.131.6 .803

4. Noor, N., Beram, S., Huat, F. K. C., Gengatharan, K., & Mohamad Rasidi, M. S. (2023). Bias, Halo Effect

and Horn Effect: A Systematic Literature Review. International Journal of Academic Research in Business and Social Sciences, 13(3). https://doi.org/10.6007/i jarbss/v13-i3/16733

5. Otake, K., Shimai, S., Tanaka-Matsumi, J., Otsui, K., & Fredrickson, B. L. (2006). Happy People Become Happier through Kindness: A Counting Kindnesses Intervention. Journal of Happiness Studies, 7(3), 361–375. https://doi.org/10.1007/s10902-005 -3650-z

6. Recency Effect - an overview | ScienceDirect Topics. (n.d.). https://www.sciencedirect.com/topics/psycho logy/recency-effect

7. Renne, B. (2018, December 28). Survey: Average person forms a first impression in just 27 seconds. Study Finds. https://studyfinds.org/survey-first-imp ression-formed-just-27-seconds

8. Turczynski, B. (2022, December 23). 2023 HR Statistics: Job Search, Hiring, Recruiting & Interviews. Zety. https://zety.com/blog/hr-statistics

About the Author

Lindsay Mustain is an award-winning CEO and the visionary behind Intentional Career Design—a professional game-changer that propels senior corporate professionals to skyrocket their annual income and is known helping professionals make 6 figure salaries (and even 6 figure increases) without going back to school and while doing work they LOVE.

With a leap of faith in 2017, Lindsay kickstarted her entrepreneurial journey by founding Talent Paradigm LLC. Her background includes 20 years in Human Resources, most recently as a recruiting leader at Amazon, where she became the company's most visible employee, reaching hundreds of millions of job seekers through her content on LinkedIn and her first book, 7 Critical Resume Mistakes to Avoid.

Intentional Career Design was created after a powerful epiphany. During Lindsay's human resources career, she reviewed more than 1,000,000 resumes, interviewed thousands of candidates, and ended up rejecting 99% of all well-qualified candidates. It was at this time that Lindsay had an epiphany moment—there had to be a better way... and she built it. Intentional Career Design amplifies corporate professional careers using the experience they already have combined with a proprietary system that beats the recruiting odds (which are less than .4%). Her clients get to stop selling their soul for a paycheck, finally go to work energized and excited, and get to make their greatest contribution while finally being rewarded financially for their genius.

Lindsay's groundbreaking strategies have supported over 20,000 clients in 121 countries across the world. Her proprietary systems and results have landed her in the limelight of renowned publications such as Business Insider, CNBC, Forbes, Entrepreneur, Create & Cultivate, The Ladders, Glassdoor, and LinkedIn.

Lindsay resides in the Emerald City (Seattle) with her family. Alongside her husband Aaron and their two delightful chil-

dren, Jacob and Nora, is a lively cast of 4 legged friends —
a half dozen feline friends (including four foster fails) and a
dynamic duo of canine companions, keeping things delightfully
interesting (and undeniably furry)!

If you'd like to work with Lindsay directly,
scan the QR code below or head to
intentionalcareerdesign.com to learn more.